ANIMALS IN OUR CARE

HORSES

Written by
Alex Hall

American adaptation copyright © 2026 by North Star Editions, Mendota Heights, MN 55120. All rights reserved. No part of this book may be reproduced or utilized in any form or by any means without written permission from the publisher.

Horses © 2024 BookLife Publishing
This edition is published by arrangement with BookLife Publishing

sales@northstareditions.com | 888-417-0195

Library of Congress Control Number:
2024952960

ISBN
978-1-952455-37-7 (library bound)
978-1-952455-93-3 (paperback)
978-1-952455-73-5 (epub)
978-1-952455-57-5 (hosted ebook)

Printed in the United States of America
Mankato, MN
092025

Written by:
Alex Hall

Edited by:
Elise Carraway

Designed by:
Ker Ker Lee

All facts, statistics, web addresses and URLs in this book were verified as valid and accurate at time of writing. No responsibility for any changes to external websites or references can be accepted by either the author or publisher.

Photo Credits – Images courtesy of Shutterstock.com, unless otherwise stated.

Cover – Eric Isselee, E LLL, Olga_i, Anaite, Lenkadan, Nynke van Holten, Rodrigo Lourezini, mariait. 2–3 – Kwadrat, Eric Isselee. 4–5 – Eric Isselee, Alexia Khruscheva, Chase D'animulls. 6–7 – Kwadrat, MrAli00, photomaster, CameraCraft. 8–9 – acceptphoto, Olga Salt, Fred van Schaagen. 10–11 – Callipso88, Vova Shevchuk. 12–13 – Chase D'animulls, Eric Isselee, mariait, GeptaYs, Osetrik, Makarova Viktoria. 14–15 – K-FK, Marian Weyo. 16–17 – giorgiomtb, schankz. 18–19 – Katho Menden, Eric Isselee. 20–21 – spatuletail, Dja65, Hanna Alandi, Piaffe Photography. 22–23 – AJP, Eric Isselee, Kwadrat, Olga_i, Chase D'animulls, STUDIO DREAM.

CONTENTS

Page 4	Horses
Page 6	The Equine Family
Page 8	Horse Faces
Page 10	Body of a Horse
Page 12	Breeds and Colors
Page 14	Caring for Your Horse
Page 16	Body Language
Page 18	From Foal to Horse
Page 20	Believe It or Not!
Page 22	Are You a Genius Kid?
Page 24	Glossary and Index

Words that look like <u>this</u> can be found in the glossary on page 24.

HORSES

Have you ever seen a horse?

Maybe you have seen a pony in a meadow or a horse in a stable.

Most horses are <u>domesticated</u>.

Horses are part of a group called the Equidae <u>family</u>. They are often known as equines.

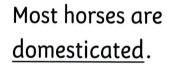

Horses are mammals. Mammals are warm-blooded, have a backbone, and make milk to feed their young. Horses are herbivores. They only eat plants.

Horses are known for being very smart animals. They have helped people do many things for thousands of years.

THE EQUINE FAMILY

Millions of years ago, there were more than 60 different animals in the equine family. However, horses, zebras, and donkeys are the only equines alive today.

Zebra

Donkey

There are some things that all equines have in common.

All animals in the equine family have manes, tails, and single-hooved feet. They have one toe on each foot.

Horses and donkeys live in many places. Wild zebras only live in Africa.

DID YOU KNOW?
All animals with hooves are called ungulates.

HORSE FACES

Let's look at the face of a horse.

Horses have some of the largest eyes of all land mammals. They can see nearly all around themselves. The only places they cannot see are straight in front and behind themselves.

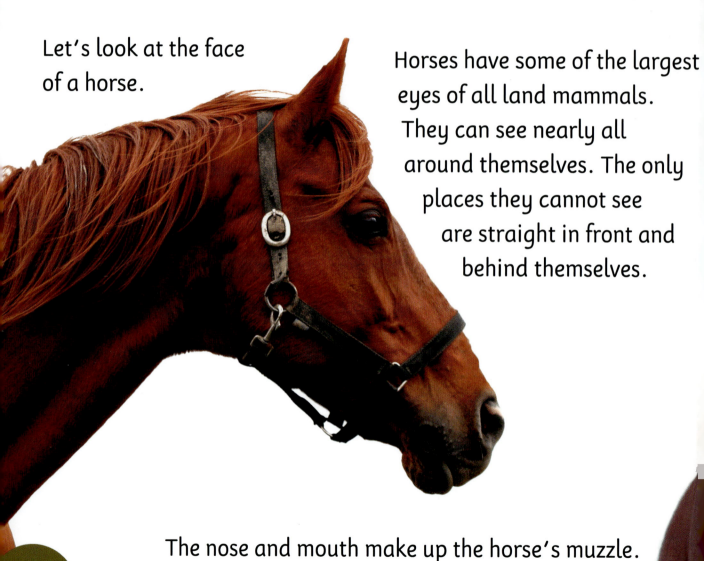

The nose and mouth make up the horse's muzzle.

Horses have long teeth that help them cut and chew food. Horses grind their teeth down by chewing a lot.

Horses have large nostrils. They can only breathe through their noses.

DID YOU KNOW?
The size of a horse's teeth can tell you how old the horse is.

BODY OF A HORSE

Horses swing their tails to keep bugs away. They also use their tails to <u>communicate</u>.

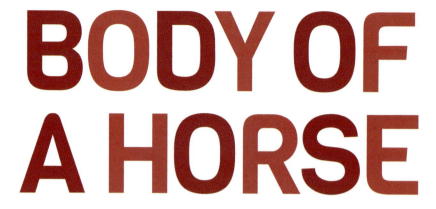

Strong legs help horses run quickly.

Horses have thick manes. Manes help keep horses warm in cold weather. Manes also protect horses from bug bites.

Each foot is covered by a hard hoof. Hooves protect the horse's toes as they run.

DID YOU KNOW?
People put metal horseshoes on horses to ride them. The horseshoes protect the hooves from the extra weight of a person.

BREEDS AND COLORS

There are many different types of horses. These types are known as breeds. Unlike wild animals that change naturally, breeds are controlled and changed by people. There are hundreds of horse breeds.

Shire

Clydesdale

Shetland pony

DID YOU KNOW?
Small horses are called ponies.

Arabian

Horses can have different colors and <u>unique</u> patterns.

Brown coat

Thoroughbred horses can be many colors, including gray, brown, and black.

Black coat

Spotted coat

Friesian horses are always black.

Appaloosa horses are always spotted.

Pinto coat

Paint horses have pinto patterns. This means they have white patches in their coat.

13

CARING FOR YOUR HORSE

Before people domesticated horses, horses were wild animals. Domesticated horses have the same natural <u>instincts</u> as wild horses. These instincts help keep them safe.

Horses may be easily frightened. It is important to be calm and patient around horses, so they do not feel scared.

Horses need plenty of grass and plants to eat. They need fresh water to drink. Horses also need exercise to stay healthy and happy.

Horses need clean stables to sleep in.

DID YOU KNOW?
A shiny mane and tail is a sign of a healthy horse.

BODY LANGUAGE

You can often tell how a horse is feeling from looking at its body. Horses may use their faces and make noises to communicate their feelings.

If a horse is scared, their eyes might be wide and on alert.

The position of a horse's tail can also show the horse's mood. A lifted tail could mean the horse is excited. A relaxed horse might have a resting tail and droopy ears.

Relaxed

Excited

FROM FOAL TO HORSE

Horses go through different stages throughout their lives.

Baby horses are called foals. Foals drink milk from their mothers. A male foal is called a colt. A female foal is called a filly.

DID YOU KNOW?
Foals can usually stand up within one hour of being born.

At one year old, foals become yearlings. Yearlings become adults around four to five years old. Adult male horses are called stallions. Females are called mares.

Mares are usually pregnant for 11 to 12 months.

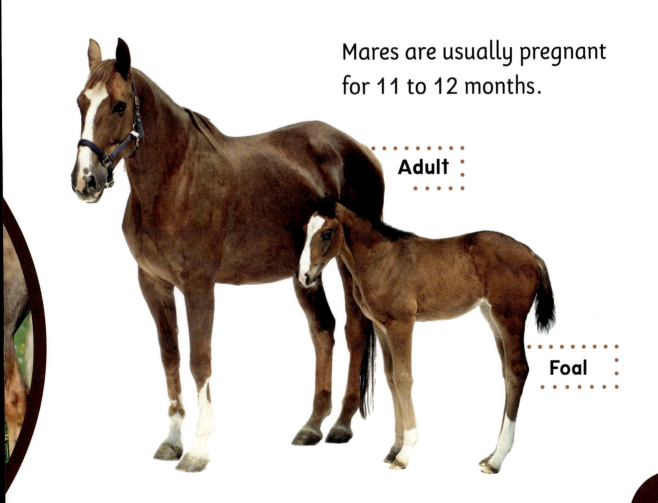

Adult

Foal

BELIEVE IT OR NOT!

Horses were first domesticated around 6,000 years ago.

Horses have helped humans in many ways. For hundreds of years, horses were used for travel. They also help on farms and ranches.

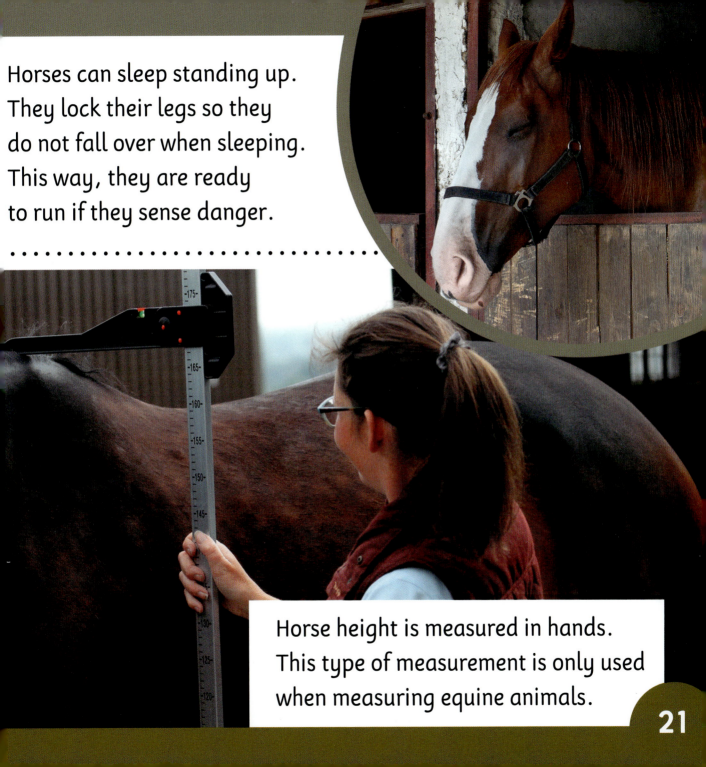

Horses can sleep standing up. They lock their legs so they do not fall over when sleeping. This way, they are ready to run if they sense danger.

Horse height is measured in hands. This type of measurement is only used when measuring equine animals.

21

ARE YOU A GENIUS KID?

You have now learned many facts about horses. Are you going to share your facts with other people? Before you do, it is time to test your knowledge to see whether you are a genius kid.

Check back through the book if you are not sure.

1. Can horses breathe through their mouths?
2. What breed of horse is always black?
3. How long ago were horses first domesticated?

Answers:
1. No. They can only breathe through their noses. 2. Friesians. 3. Around 6,000 years ago.

GLOSSARY

communicate   to pass information between two or more things

domesticated   when an animal isn't wild and is taken care of by humans

family   a way of grouping animals with very similar traits

instincts   natural patterns of behaviors in animals

unique   one of a kind or very rare

INDEX

eyes 8, 16
foals 18–19
hooves 7, 11
legs 10, 21
manes 7, 11, 15

mares 19
noses 8–9, 23
stallions 19
tails 7, 10, 15, 17
toes 7, 11